I LOVE YOU MORE THAN...

written by **Lubna Kharusi**
illustrated by **Amir** and **Meliha Al-Zubi**

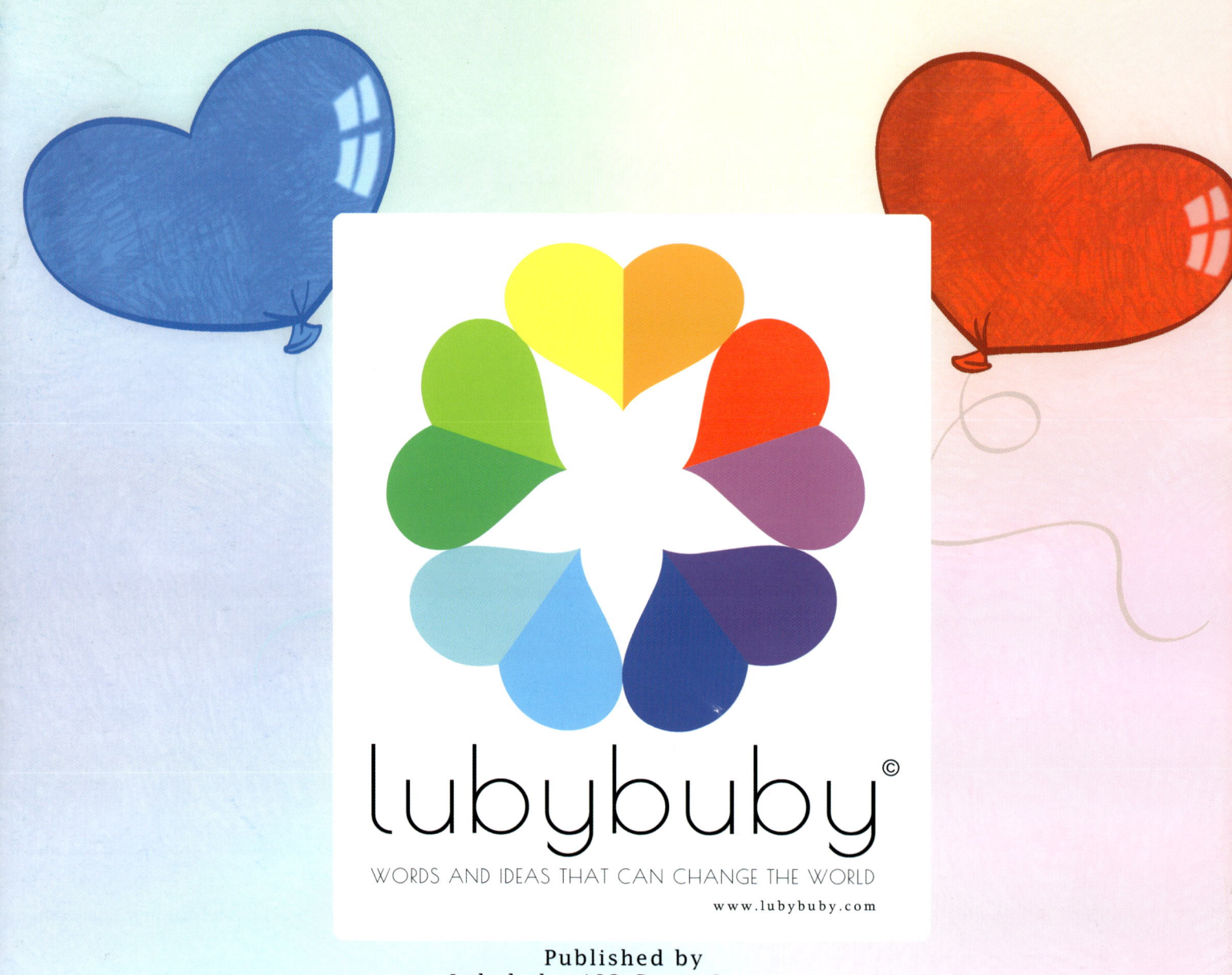

lubybuby

WORDS AND IDEAS THAT CAN CHANGE THE WORLD

www.lubybuby.com

Published by
Lubybuby 483 Green Lanes,
London, N13 4BS, UK,
www.lubybuby.com
ISBN 978-0-9930901-2-7
I Love You More Than...-A Picture Dictionary
All rights reserved.
No part of this book may be produced in any form
without written permission from the author.
Copyright© Lubna Kharusi 2014.

This book is based on a game I use to play with my daughters when we were living in London.

We would think of things to finish off the sentence "I love you more than...".

This book also includes a picture dictionary that is associated with the sentence, so they can increase their vocabulary in a loving environment.

I find the best teacher is love, and it is my children who taught me what love really means.

Lubna Kharusi

I LOVE YOU MORE THAN MY ARMS CAN REACH

 HUG  STAR  SKYSCRAPER  FIREWORKS  FOUNTAIN

I LOVE YOU MORE THAN ALL THE SAND ON THE BEACH

 HAT
 CRAB
 BUCKET
 STARFISH
 SANDCASTLE

I LOVE YOU MORE THAN ALL THE STARS IN THE SKY

MERCURY · VENUS · MARS · JUPITER · SATURN · URANUS · NEPTUNE

EARTH

 MOON

 PLANET

 SHOOTING STAR

 TELESCOPE

 SPACESHIP

I LOVE YOU MORE THAN ALL THE DAYS GONE BY

CAKE

GIFT

BALLOON

CANDLE

PARTY HAT

I LOVE YOU MORE THAN ALL THE BUBBLES IN A BATH

BATH

CAT

SOAP

BUBBLE

SHAMPOO

I LOVE YOU MORE THAN ALL THE NUMBERS THERE ARE IN MATHS

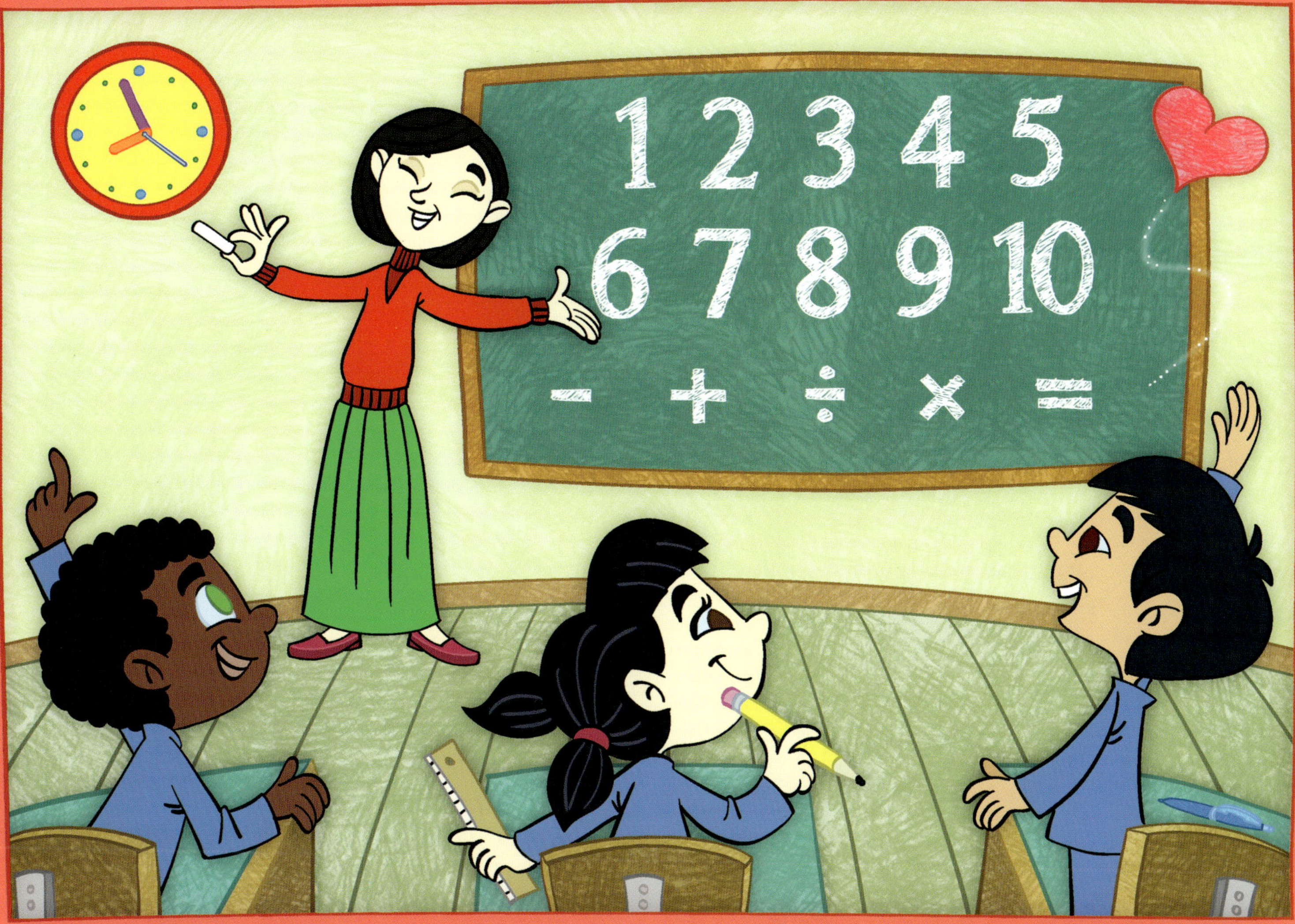

 PEN

 PENCIL

 TABLE

 RULER

 BLACKBOARD

I LOVE YOU MORE THAN ALL THE FOOD THERE IS TO EAT

 FORK

 SPOON

 KNIFE

 PLATE

 GLASS

I LOVE YOU MORE THAN FUN IN SUMMER'S HEAT

 SUN

 GRASS

 PICNIC

 CHIPMUNK

 LADYBIRD

I LOVE YOU MORE THAN DANCING IN THE POURING RAIN

 RAIN

 BOOT

 PUDDLE

 COAT

 UMBRELLA

I LOVE YOU MORE THAN ALL THE SNOWFLAKES OUTSIDE MY WINDOWPANE

COOKIE

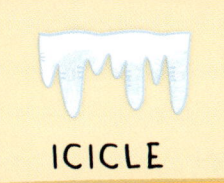

ICICLE

SNOWMAN

SNOWFLAKE

FIREPLACE

I LOVE YOU MORE THAN ALL OF THE FISH IN THE SEA

FISH   SHELL   SHARK   MERMAID   OCTOPUS

I LOVE YOU MORE THAN ALL THE CARS THAT GO WHEEEEEE

 CAR
 ROAD
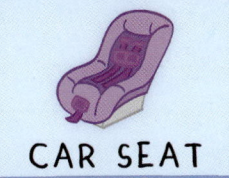 CAR SEAT
 TIRE
 TRUCK

I LOVE YOU MORE THAN ALL THE COUNTRIES IN THE WORLD

 CAMERA

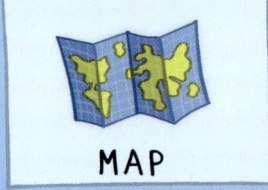 MAP

 BAG

 PASSPORT

 SUITCASE

I LOVE YOU MORE THAN
ALL THE TREASURES OF DIAMONDS AND PEARLS

SHIP

PIRATE

PARROT

PRINCESS

TREASURE

I LOVE YOU MORE THAN ALL THE LEAVES IN THE AMAZON

FROG

SNAKE

SPIDER

BUTTERFLY

TOUCAN

I LOVE YOU MORE THAN ALL THE NOTES IN A FAMILIAR SONG

 CONDUCTOR
 PIANO
 TRUMPET
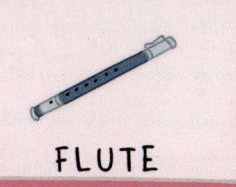 FLUTE
 VIOLIN

I LOVE YOU MORE THAN ALL THE DREAMS THAT I CAN DREAM

BED   PILLOW   ROBOT   BLANKET   TEDDY BEAR

I LOVE YOU MORE THAN MY FAVOURITE WINNING SPORTS TEAM

 NET

 BALL

 SOCKS

 SHORTS

 SNEAKERS

I LOVE YOU MORE THAN A COLOURFUL RAINBOW OF LIGHT

CLOUD

RABBIT

RAINBOW

PAINTING

PAINT BRUSH

I LOVE YOU MORE THAN EVERYTHING IN MY SIGHT

 LION  GIRAFFE  ZEBRA  ELEPHANT  LEOPARD

I LOVE YOU MORE THAN MY YOUTHFUL DAYS

BABY BOY GIRL MAN WOMAN

I LOVE YOU MORE THAN FAIRIES AND THEIR MAGICAL WAYS

 OWL

 WAND

 FAIRY

 WIZARD

 WINGS

I LOVE YOU MORE THAN ALL THE AIR THERE IS TO BREATHE

 KITE
 LEAF
 GRAPES
 TREE
 FLOWER

I LOVE YOU MORE THAN ANYTHING I COULD EVER NEED

 RING
 SHOES
 DRESS
 CROWN 
 NECKLACE

I LOVE YOU MORE THAN ALL THE LETTERS AND WORDS I KNOW

 APPLE

 LAMP

 GLASSES

 BOOK

 CHAIR

I LOVE YOU FROM THE TOP OF YOUR HEAD TO THE TIP OF YOUR TOES

 EYE
 NOSE
 MOUTH
 HAND
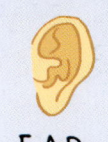 EAR

I LOVE YOU MORE THAN ALL THE POSSIBLE SHAPES THERE ARE

		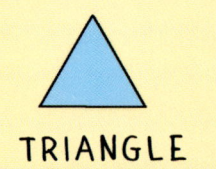		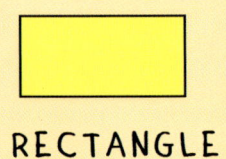
CIRCLE	SQUARE	TRIANGLE	HEART	RECTANGLE

I LOVE YOU WHEREVER I AM, NEAR OR FAR

LETTER

MOBILE

LAPTOP

AIRPLANE

BOAT

I LOVE YOU MORE THAN ALL THE ANIMALS IN A ZOO

 BIRD
 TIGER
 KOALA
 MONKEY
 CROCODILE

I'LL LOVE YOU ALWAYS, NO MATTER WHAT YOU DO

DOG

MOTHER

FATHER

SON

DAUGHTER

I LOVE YOU MORE THAN

lubybuby
WORDS AND IDEAS THAT CAN CHANGE THE WORLD

Purchase our other AMAZING BOOKS!
Download free Music & Videos from www.lubybuby.com

Made of Love by Lubna Kharusi
Illustrated by Amir and Meliha Al-Zubi
Music by Hakely Nakao Chavez, Thanae Pachiyannakis and Lubna Kharusi

Fly My Little Butterfly by Lubna Kharusi
Illustrations by Amir and Meliha Al-Zubi

www.lubybuby.com